MAKE ME LAUGH!

THE SKY'S THE LIMIT

NATURALLY FUNNY JOKES

by Rick and Ann Walton with Scott K.
Peterson and Peter and Connie Roop
pictures by Brian Gable

Carolrhoda Books, Inc. • Minneapolis

Q: What kind of coats do trees wear?
A: Douglas firs.

Q: What flowers live in pickle jars?
A: Daffo-dills.

Q: Where should you keep the wind?
A: In an air pocket.

Q: What is a tree's favorite fruit?
A: Pineapple.

Q: What kind of salad do snowmen eat?
A: Cold-slaw.

Q: What do space squirrels like to eat?
A: Astro-nuts.

Q: Why do pine trees buy only ice cream?
A: Because they already have the cones.

Q: What do snowmen put on their faces to keep them looking young?
A: Cold cream.

Q: What do snowmen put on their faces to keep them looking even younger?
A: Ice cream.

Q: What kind of plant likes gymnastics?
A: A tumbleweed.

Q: Why shouldn't you wear snowshoes?
A: Because they'll melt.

Q: What do you get when you cross a barn with a pine tree?

A: A needle in a haystack.

Q: Why did the tree pack her trunk?

A: Because she was leafing town.

Q: If an athlete gets athlete's foot, what does an astronaut get?

A: Missile-toe.

Q: Why are snowmen careful not to get into trouble?

A: Because they don't want to be in hot water.

Q: Why do windows have panes?

A: Because the rain beats on them.

Q: Why was the spruce tree so sad?

A: Because she was a blue spruce.

Q: Why didn't the tree play checkers?

A: Because she was a chess-nut.

Q: What do you get if you're hit by an icicle?

A: A cold sore.

Q: What did the sun say to the snowman?

A: "I thaw you!"

Q: What do well-dressed snowmen wear?

A: Snowsuits.

Q: Why did the sheriff put the star in jail?

A: It was a shooting star.

Q: What kind of flowers can you find in zoos?

A: Tiger lilies.

Q: What flowers talk during April and May?

A: Two lips.

Q: What did one maple tree say to the other?

A: "You sure are a sap."

Q: How do you know when a snowstorm is saying good-bye?

A: You can see a cold wave.

Q: What can you catch if you go ice fishing?

A: A cold.

Q: What should you wear if you want to go out in a hailstorm?

A: A hail-met.

Q: Why did the woman bury all her change in the garden?

A: She wanted to have rich soil for her plants.

Q: What does the sun drink out of?

A: Sunglasses.

Q: What kind of trees do Gypsies read?

A: Palm trees.

Q: What do clouds wear when it gets cold?

A: Raincoats.

Q: What do clouds wear under their raincoats?

A: Thunder-wear.

Q: What are the best days for astronauts to go into space?

A: Moon-day and Saturn-day.

Q: What's the hardest storm to sweep up?

A: A dust storm.

Q: What holds up the moon?

A: Moonbeams.

Q: What kind of dog floats in the air?

A: An Airedale.

Q: What do you get if an Airedale floats too near the sun?

A: A hot dog.

Q: Why did the astronaut take a mop into space?

A: To clean up the stardust.

Q: How do trees clap?

A: With their palms.

Q: What flower has the best eyesight?

A: The iris.

Q: Where should you keep your clouds?

A: In a cloud bank.

Q: Why was the tree wearing sunglasses and carrying a towel?

A: Because he was a beech tree.

Q: What's the weather always like at parades?

A: Partly crowdy.

Q: What goes up when you count down?

A: A rocket.

Q: How did the corn plant lose all her money?

A: By playing the stalk market.

Q: How do you lock a storm door?

A: With a thunderbolt.

Q: Why did the tree want to be a jeweler?

A: Because he had so many rings.

Q: What kind of years weigh the least?

A: Light years.

Q: Where can you buy a storm?

A: From a storm cellar.

Q: What kind of flowers can you find in space?

A: Sunflowers.

Q: Why are trees so successful?

A: Because they are always reaching new heights.

Q: What does the sun eat off of?

A: A hot plate.

Q: How can you tell if it's going to rain cats and dogs?

A: The wind will begin to howl.

Q: What's the temperature like when it rains cats and dogs?

A: It's biting cold.

Q: Why wouldn't the banker give the tree a loan?

A: Because she didn't want to go out on a limb.

Q: Why did the twigs go to Washington?

A: Because they wanted to belong to different branches of the government.

Q: What knocks down houses and makes people laugh?

A: A cy-clown.

Q: Why did the cow jump over the moon?

A: To get to the Milky Way.

Q: Why didn't the maple trust the oak tree?

A: Because the oak looked a little shady.

Q: What did Mr. and Mrs. Tree name their son?

A: Woodrow.

Q: Why are flowers such good friends?

A: Because they started out as buds.

Q: Why did the astronaut take a shovel into space?

A: To dig a black hole.

Q: How do you hold up the sky during the daytime?

A: With sunbeams.

Q: Why do thin cowboys make good astronauts?

A: They're good at sitting in a saddle-light.

Q: Where do trees keep their luggage?

A: In their trunks.

Q: When is the earth cleanest?

A: Right after it showers.

Q: Why should stars wear braces?

A: Because there's so much space between them.

Q: Why are vines so lazy?

A: Because all they want to do is hang around.

Q: What's the best way to keep from getting wet when you go outside?

A: Don't go out when it's raining.

Q: How does an astronaut keep up his pants?

A: With an asteroid belt!

Q: What did one shrub say to the other shrub?

A: "I'm bushed."

Q: What do you get when a cloudburst hits a flock of ducks?

A: A downpour.

Q: Why doesn't Mother Nature cover the grass in water every morning?

A: She doesn't want to over-dew it.

Q: Where do Martians go fishing?

A: In the galax-seas.

Q: Why didn't the satellite go very far?

A: It kept going around in circles.

Q: What happened to the tree who came home late?

A: He was grounded.

Q: What's stranger than when it rains cats and dogs?

A: When kings rain.

Q: What's even stranger than kings raining?

A: Baby showers.

Q: How is a telephone like the planet Saturn?

A: They both have rings.

Q: What tree tires easily?

A: A rubber tree.

Q: Why did the astronaut take an American flag into space?

A: It was a star-spangled banner.

Q: What flower is the king of the garden?

A: The dandy-lion.

Q: Why don't flowers talk?

A: Because it's hard to get them to open up.

Q: Why was the bush always fibbing?

A: Because she was a lie-lac.

Q: What makes a cloudburst?

A: A windbreaker.

Q: What's an astronaut's favorite fish?

A: Starfish.

Q: How does the man in the moon cut his hair?

A: Eclipse-it.

Q: Why is the sun a welcome guest at parties?

A: Because the sun knows how to break the ice.

Q: What's the difference between fog and a falling star?

A: One is mist on earth, and the other is missed in space.

Q: Why are acorns so obnoxious?

A: Because they are always acting like nuts.

Q: Why did the singer go up into space?

A: She wanted to become a star.

Q: Why did the plant go on stage?

A: He wanted to be under the lights.

Q: What do space toads have all over their bodies?

A: Star warts!

Q: Why is the sun so bright?

A: Because it has millions of degrees.

Q: What did the Egyptians call their flowers?

A: Mum-mies.

Q: Why didn't the girl flower go out with the boy flower?

A: Because he never aster.

Q: When do you know that the weather's sad?

A: When you hear the wind wailing.

Q: What do snowmen ride?

A: Ice-cycles.

Q: Where do astronauts go to college?

A: UFO—University for Orbiting.

Q: Why can't you find a comb in a jungle?

A: Because there is so much brush.

Q: What time is it when a Martian peeks in your window?

A: Time to close the blinds!

Q: What do you get when you cross the sun with a goose?

A: Sundown.

Q: Why did the tree take a bath?

A: Because she wanted to spruce herself up.

Q: How can you tell when two vines are in love?

A: Because they are always clinging to each other.

Q: How do trees relax?

A: They get together and shoot the breeze.

Q: What's the best way to shoot the breeze?

A: With an air rifle.

Q: What kind of shots do astronauts get?

A: Boosters.

Q: What does the breeze blow?

A: Wind instruments.

Q: Why do astronauts enjoy space travel?

A: It's out of this world!

Q: Why is thunder so noisy?

A: Because it uses a cloud-speaker.

Q: What are clouds' favorite wind instruments?

A: Foghorns.

Q: What's the best way to talk to a Martian?

A: By long distance!

Q: What did the North Star say to the Big Dipper?

A: "It's not polite to point!"

Q: How do you protect yourself from an angry windstorm.

A: With a windshield.

Q: How do you know when the moon isn't hungry?

A: When it's full!

Q: What kind of music do astronauts like?

A: Nep-tunes.

Q: Why couldn't the trees figure out the riddle?

A: Because they were all stumped.

Q: What's the difference between a thunderstorm and a sore lion?

A: One pours with rain, while the other roars with pain.

Q: Who saves clouds from danger?

A: Thunderdog.

Q: What does the runner-up in the Ms. Galaxy contest receive?

A: A constellation prize.

Q: Why don't some people like trees?

A: Because they think that trees are for the birds.

Q: What do you get when you cross a snowstorm with a cornfield?

A: Cornflakes.

Q: Which astronaut goes into space the most?

A: Sir Launch-a-lot.

Q: Why do snow shovelers make a lot of money?

A: Because there's no business like snow business.

Q: What do you find in a snowbank?

A: Cold cash.

Q: What do you get when you cross an evergreen tree with a pig?

A: A porky-pine.

Q: Why can't a Martian's nose be twelve inches long?

A: If it were, it would be a foot!

Q: Why shouldn't you go up in the sky during a heavy storm?

A: Because it's already overclouded.

Q: Why is there always a kitten by the swamp?

A: Because he's looking for his cattails.

Q: What do you get if you put a mousetrap in your freezer?

A: A cold snap.

Q: Why wouldn't the tree settle down in one spot?

A: Because she was made of driftwood.

Q: What did one tree say to the other?

A: I think it's time we split.

Q: How did the first person ever hit by lightning feel?

A: Shocked.

Q: How do old storms travel fast?

A: They use hurrycanes.

Q: Why did the trees bow?

A: Because the thunder clapped.

Q: How do you capture a fly from outer space?

A: Use a Venus flytrap.

Q: What tree has the most bark?
A: A dogwood.

Q: Who is the king of winter?
A: Old King Cold.

Q: What does Old King Cold do?
A: He rains.

Q: Where does Old King Cold live?
A: Castles in the air.

Q: How can animals tell what the weather's going to be like?
A: They look at the fur-cast.

Q: Where do nice children plant flowers?
A: In a kinder-garden.

Q: What do cats like to do in the winter?
A: Go mice skating.

This book is available in two editions:
Library binding by Carolrhoda Books, Inc.,
  a division of Lerner Publishing Group
Soft cover by First Avenue Editions,
  an imprint of Lerner Publishing Group
241 First Avenue North
Minneapolis, MN 55401 U.S.A.

Website address: www.carolrhodabooks.com

Library of Congress Cataloging-in-Publication Data

    The sky's the limit : naturally funny jokes / by Rick Walton [et al.] ; pictures by Brian Gable.
        p.   cm. — (Make me laugh!)
    Summary: Presents a variety of jokes about nature.
    ISBN: 1–57505–663–1 (lib. bdg. : alk. paper)
    ISBN: 1–57505–735–2 (pbk. : alk. paper)
        1. Wit and humor, Juvenile. 2. Nature—Juvenile humor. [1. Nature—Humor.
    2. Jokes.] I. Walton, Rick. II. Gable, Brian, 1949– ill. III. Series.
    PN6166.S58 2005
    818'.60208—dc22   2003019245

Manufactured in the United States of America
1 2 3 4 5 6 — DP — 10 09 08 07 06 05

MAKE ME LAUGH!

REAL CLASSY

SILLY SCHOOL JOKES

by Rick and Ann Walton with John Jansen
pictures by Brian Gable

🎵 Carolrhoda Books, Inc. • Minneapolis

Q: Why did the fish go to school?

A: He heard they had bookworms.

Q: Where did the math student eat lunch?

A: At the multiplication table.

Q: What do you get if you're allergic to the letter *B*?

A: B-hives.

Q: Why did the math student bring a ruler to bed?

A: She wanted to see how long she slept.

Q: What's the best way to shoot an L-shaped arrow?

A: With an L-bow.

Q: Where did the student write his poems?

A: Under the poet-tree.

Q: Why did the student bring his glasses home?

A: To study for the eye test.

Q: Why should you throw an *S* at a cat if you want it to go away?

A: Because it will make the cat SCAT.

Q: What color did the art teacher paint the sun and wind?

A: He painted the sun rose and the wind blue.

Q: Why do *O* and *M* like each other?

A: Because they have so much in COMMON.

Q: Did the teacher write with his left or right hand?

A: Neither. He wrote with a pencil.

Q: How should you feel if a letter *N* gives you a pat on the back?

A: N-couraged.

Q: What letters of the alphabet should you stay away from?

A: *N M E.*

Q: What did the science teachers say was at the center of Earth?

A: The letter *R.*

Q: Why are there so few letter *Q*s in the dictionary?

A: Because *Q* is not in DEMAND.

Q: What did the witch teach in school?

A: Spelling.

Q: What did the letter *T* say to the pencil?

A: "You've crossed me for the last time!"

Q: Where do baby cows eat their school lunches?

A: In the calf-eteria.

Q: Why is the letter *A* at the head of the alphabet?

A: Because it's in CHARGE.

Q: Where do you eat lunch if you have a cold?

A: In the cough-eteria.

Q: Why did the alligator do well in school?

A: He always gave snappy answers.

Q: Why did the teacher need glasses?

A: She had bad pupils.

Q: What letter is always in hot water?

A: *T.*

Q: What did the school janitor say when the kids asked him about his job?

A: "It's picking up."

Q: Why was the chess team in the dark?

A: They lost all their matches.

Q: Why did the teacher wear sunglasses?

A: Her students were very bright.

Q: What is the capital of France?

A: The letter *F.*

Q: What's the best way to catch a school of fish?

A: With bookworms.

Q: When did the American patriots celebrate a letter?

A: At the Boston *T* Party.

Q: Why were there only twenty-four letters in the alphabet two hundred years ago?

A: Because U and I weren't there.

Q: How do we know Hamlet had trouble spelling rabbit?

A: Because he asked himself, "Two *B*s or not two *B*s."

Q: How do scholars get across the sea?

A: They use scholarships.

Q: What should you feed the letter *C*?

A: C-food.

Q: What's black when it's clean and white when it's dirty?

A: A chalkboard.

MLE: "How did you feel when you got a D on your test?"

KT: "D-graded!"

Q: Where did the teacher grow her vegetables?

A: In the kinder-garden.

Q: Why did the students wear sunglasses?

A: It was an illuminating lesson.

Q: What two letters are all right?
A: OK.

Q: Why did the report card sting?
A: It was all Bs.

Q: How would you feel if you ate a lot of *P*s?
A: *P*s-full.

Q: Why does the letter *Z* frequently get lost?

A: Because it's always in a HAZE.

Q: What did the student have just before he got his report card?

A: Grade Expectations.

Q: What did the teacher say when the student wrote *WETHR*?

A: "That's the worst spell of weather we've seen in a long time."

Q: What do you find twice as much of in nighttime as in daytime?

A: The letter *T*.

Q: Which letter is magical?

A: The Fair-E.

Q: Was the student in a bad mood during finals?

A: No, he was just a little testy.

Q: Why did the student give his report card a parachute?

A: Because all his grades were falling.

Q: Why did the naughty student hang around school?

A: Because he was suspended.

Q: What happened when the *J* suddenly came onto the baseball field?

A: It made the ump JUMP.

Q: Why will the letter *A* send food into space?

A: Because it will make your lunch LAUNCH.

Q: Why don't spies like the letter *S*?

A: Because it makes their lip SLIP.

Q: How did the writer get across the water?

A: She took the penmanship.

Q: What did the astronomy student get for taking second place?

A: The constellation prize.

Q: Why should you never eat a treat that has the letter *H* on it?

A: Because it makes the treat a THREAT.

Q: Why is an *E* a welcome sight to a hungry person?

A: Because it turns a fast into a FEAST.

Q: Why did the student hate learning about Egypt?

A: She was in denial.

Q: How do you feel if a giant letter *D* sits on you?

A: D-pressed.

Q: What did the science teacher say when she was asked, "Which is faster, heat or cold?"

A: She said "Heat, because you can catch cold."

Q: Why was the geometry teacher so confusing?

A: Because he talked in circles.

Q: Why was the math student afraid of the number 7?

A: Because 7 8 9.

Q: Why did the teacher go to the beach?

A: He wanted to test the waters.

Q: Who haunts the school?

A: The school spirit.

Q: Why should you take an *R* away from Fred if he's hungry?

A: Because it gets Fred FED.

Q: Why should you give the letter *R* to a fiend?

A: Because it will make the fiend a FRIEND.

Q: Why should you never put an *S* on a lime?

A: Because it makes the lime SLIME.

Q: What did the vampire learn in school?

A: Punctur-ation.

Q: Why do uncles and aunts like to take the letter *E* away from a naughty niece?

A: Because they know that it will make their niece NICE.

Q: Why did the skeleton skip school?

A: It didn't have the guts for it.

Q: Why did Dracula go to school?

A: He was looking for the alpha-bat.

Q: Why are the letters *T* and *E* so popular?

A: Because they're always in STYLE and never out of DATE.

Q: Where did the ghost go to learn?

A: High ghoul.

Q: Why did the girl break her leg before the school play?

A: She wanted to be in the cast.

Q: Why did the science teacher bring a chicken to school?

A: Her class was doing eggs-periments.

Q: Why are *L* and *I* so straight?

A: Because everyone keeps them in LINE.

Q: Why does Nat's mother like the letter *E*?

A: Because it makes Nat NEAT.

Q: What happens when Ben gets hit by a letter *T*?

A: Ben becomes BENT.

Q: What do you get if someone hits you with a letter *I*?

A: An I-sore.

Q: What do you get when you cross a professor and a monster?

A: The Teacher from the Black Lagoon.

Q: What letter reminds you of looking in the mirror?

A: *W*.

Q: Why is the letter *S* easy to recognize?

A: Because it appears everywhere in PERSON.

Q: Why was it smooth sailing with the report card?

A: It was nothing but straight Cs.

Q: How do you feel if the letter *N* puts a curse on you?

A: N-chanted.

Q: When is a report card like a sheep?

A: When the grades are B-A-A-B-A-A.

Q: Why couldn't the bookworm sneeze?

A: He had his nose in a book.

Q: Why are the letters *L* and *O* so close?

A: Because they're in LOVE.

Q: Who scared the students in the hall?

A: The Lockerness monster.

Q: What book is a good listener?

A: The school 'earbook.

Q: Why should a kid never carry the letter *S* while he's walking on ice?

A: Because it'll make the kid SKID.

Q: Why was the math book so sad?

A: It was full of problems.

Q: Why will the letter *C* never go straight?

A: Because it goes in CIRCLES.

Q: Why was the student afraid to go to school?

A: She didn't want to get stung by the spelling bee.

Q: How did the spelling bee champion correct the word "Beee?"

A: She used an eraser.

Q: What do you get when you cross the letter *M* with the king of cats?

A: The M-purr-er.

Q: Why should you never get in a plane with a letter *T*?

A: Because it will turn the plane into a PLANET.

Q: Why did the school add another floor of English classes?

A: They wanted another story.

Q: How did the music teacher want his students to play?

A: Solo. Solo they couldn't be heard.

Q: Why can the letter *T* run forever?

A: Because it's always in CONDITION and never out of BREATH.

Q: Why was the teacher unpopular?

A: He had no class.

Q: What are there four of in every engine but never found in any car?

A: The letter *E*.

Q: If you want to see a lot of letter *D*s, what should you do?

A: Take a D-tour.

Q: Why did the king go to school?

A: He heard they needed a ruler.

Q: What letter will give you a lift?

A: The L-evator.

Q: Why is an extra *A* a nice thing for someone to have?

A: It turns any place into a PALACE.

Q: What letter likes to swing?

A: The chimpan-Z.

Q: What letter is a game for birds?

A: Crow-K.

Q: How boring was the teacher?

A: He even made the chalk bored.

Q: What was the teacher's favorite dessert?
A: Edu-cake.

Q: What's the best way to shine the letter *B*?
A: With *B*s-wax.

Q: What letter is difficult to figure out?
A: Mister-E.

Q: Why did the dogs go to school?

A: They heard there was going to be a pup rally.

Q: Why should you always carry a *W* with you if you're in a hurry?

A: Because it will make your heels WHEELS.

Q: What do you get if you plant a letter *C*?

A: C-weed.

Q: What three letters do athletes like?

A: *N R G.*

Q: Why was the best-liked teacher also the coolest?

A: Because she had lots of fans.

Q: Where do teachers send students who don't tell the truth?

A: To the lie-brary.

Q: Why are the letters *B* and *D* like a beach?

A: Because they're found next to the C.

Q: How happy was everybody when school finally ended?

A: Even the hands on the clocks applauded.

Q: What letters perform in the circus?

A: The trap-Es.

Q: Why is the letter *V* never late?

A: Because it always shows up in ADVANCE.

Q: Where does the letter *C* go swimming?

A: At the C-shore.

Q: What do you need for music class?

A: A notebook.

Q: How did the gym teacher travel?

A: She went coach.

Q: Who was the best athlete in school?

A: Jim Class.

Q: What do beginning fishers have to learn?

A: Their alpha-bait.

Q: Why was the report card all wet?

A: All the grades were below C level.

Q: What can you always find in the middle of the night?

A: The letter *G*.

Q: Why can't you whisper in school?

A: Because it isn't aloud.

Q: Why doesn't the letter *H* get any visitors?

A: Because it's in the middle of NOWHERE.

Q: What will we see at the end of time?

A: The letter *E.*

Q: Why did the classroom stink?

A: It was full of pew-pils.

Q: What's the difference between an angler and a bad student?

A: One baits his hooks, the other hates his books.

Q: What should you do if you accidentally drop your letter *C* down a well?

A: Go deep-C fishing.

Q: What's bacteria?

A: The rear entrance to the cafeteria.

GG: "How did you feel when you stuck the *D* in the lamp?"

DD: "D-lighted!"

Q: Why is it easy to see the letter *E*?

A: Because it's at the end of your NOSE.

Q: What do beginning gamblers have to learn?

A: Their alphabet.

Q: Why is the letter *L* healthy?

A: Because all's well that ends WELL.

This book is available in two editions:
Library binding by Carolrhoda Books, Inc.,
  a division of Lerner Publishing Group
Soft cover by First Avenue Editions,
  an imprint of Lerner Publishing Group
241 First Avenue North
Minneapolis, MN 55401 U.S.A.

Website address: www.carolrhodabooks.com

Library of Congress Cataloging-in-Publication Data

Walton, Rick.
    Real classy : silly school jokes / by Rick and Ann Walton with John Jansen ;
  pictures by Brian Gable.
      p.   cm. — (Make me laugh)
    Summary: A collection of jokes about school and education.
    ISBN: 1–57505–665–8 (lib. bdg. : alk. paper)
    ISBN: 1–57505–740–9 (pbk. : alk. paper)
    1. Schools—Juvenile humor. 2. Education—Juvenile humor. [1. Jokes. 2.
  Riddles. 3. Schools—Humor.] I. Walton, Ann, 1963– II. Jansen, John, 1956–
  III. Gable, Brian, 1949– ill. IV. Title. V. Series.
  PN6231.S3W33 2005
  818'.5402—dc22   2003019355

Manufactured in the United States of America
1 2 3 4 5 6 — DP — 10 09 08 07 06 05